Finding Freud

〜

Finding Freud

Poems by

Tyler Norris

Kelsay Books

Cover: (by *Dannysoar* @ flikr)

ISBN: 13-978-1-945752-81-0

Kelsay Books
Aldrich Press
www.kelsaybooks.com

For Father, Mother,
and above all, Myself

Acknowledgments

The Talon Review: "We Called it Our House"

Contents

Oedipus

About the Author

Father

Mio Padre

I wonder what I should call you,
this dull flame in the shape of a man
resting in the shadows of my childhood.
That was where I left you
after all, your name coming in
and out of my mother's lips,
resting on my ears like a living seed,
growing in the back of my mind
each day, bulbous and ugly-
kicking violently at the impulse
to expand outward, to push
out of those dark chambers
and breathe
so that name could look into my face
and finally call me its father.

I take after you, old man,
and so I looked forward even
when its eyes were wide
behind me, a child of my own,
imagining the geometry of my face.
The only difference between us
was my recognition of the possibility
that I might hear that child's voice
at my front door one day,
fully mature and wanting,
and when it opens its lips to speak
it will speak that word, that name,
the only artifact of myself I left behind,
and when I face the infant that you left in me
I will embrace it, and call it my own.
I will become the father of my own initiative,
the father that you chose not to be.

My Father

There was a calculation
in your every step,
even when you signed
the papers to make me
your child.

You sported
your achievements
on your cufflinks,
hardly uttering a noise

about gunfire, or the iron
arm of the law coming down
on each and every name
they lay before you.

Your fist was a tranquil ghost,
though I never had that
spirited nature, a fire
for combat, as you did,

fighting from the bush;
a career position's name
was just another target-
a means to another end,

the way you looked at it,
as you climbed from one
title to the next,
hungry to see the realization

of the law.

The military, the State;
you worked through the ranks
of both, carrying your achievements
on your back like a wounded soldier,

yet your jacket lie naked
by the hand of your superiors.
You preferred it that way,
and I fought you for it,

but what I could never see
through the glass of your perspective
was the weight you carried
on your shoulders every day,

the way your name stuck like a bullet
in the hearts of politicians whose titles
turned blue with privilege,
the way they averted their gaze

in the wake of your walk,
a salute to their shameful character
in the presence of a leader
among general men.

Sarah's Triptych: *Sun*

The setting sun weighs its softened
orange glow over the scene like
waves before a sandy beach and he wonders
about the words he has been searching to say.

Here they are, like crabs, lying
side by side beneath the palm trees,
and she has fallen asleep in the warmth
of the enveloping scene.

Do you know the way the water moves,
the way it mouths its quiet message
to the shore? It moves independently
from the sand and sky, but is only known
by the gravity that loves it.

As he lies next to her, he says his speech
to her distant mind. The way she breathes
is like counting the colorful shells laid
out for miles in the sand, one
after the other.

The relief that comes from saying his thought
is met by a lonely wind; the two of them meet with
a silent understanding. The sun creeps its way
toward the horizon, losing its color each second.
The sun has made its proclamation: its story is
the day that it has made for all the people living
on Earth. Without a word, all its prestige

vanishes from the world, condemned
by the schedule that owns it.

He is owned by the schedule of her heart
as he watches over her sleeping breast, yet the sun
has spoken better words than anything
he has ever said to her, awake or sleeping. As the sky
begins to darken, her light begins to grow
as her eyes slowly open.

To My Brother I

I can see where you're headed
from my position out on the bleachers,
the way the ball shifts from black
to white in its spinning rotation-
the way the boys fall behind
in your every sprinting step,
and you turn their cheeks to roses
the way the sun turns the seasons
in earnest,

but the field's blowing a bitter wind
from where I'm sitting, the way you twist
ankles with the assistant coach during
practice drills, the way your skill improves,
the way he carries you on his shoulders
after every winning game.

Do you call him brother?

Banging steel resonates isolated
in a midnight gym as I add
five more pounds to a second set,
pressing repetitions into every
beading laceration of effort.
The shred muscle tissue
is like the gap between your sports,
and my artistic stage;
but I always read responsibility
like a script when I was around you,
and I find myself wondering
if there was ever a line about love
that I was meant to have spoken
into the audience of your little heart?

450 Lbs

It was the sound of metal
on rusted metal, the crashing of iron
like a boxing bell ringing.

My fight
had started at an early age
when the anxiety of hitting a ball ran circles
around my mind like the bases
on a diamond, or repeated doses of medication
that fortified my every excuse.

A breathing treatment
can't keep the bread off a dinner tray-
a hunger that ate away at my position on the field
and in the esteem of athletic men.

The weight I had gained pushed opportunity into
other arms, a burden that clung to me in the bedroom
even after the wind had blown women
in different directions, and I found myself
burying my frustration in the mouths
of the very same-
a collection that bare no
satisfaction like the motivation that followed:
a subscription to my own endeavors, a weight
being lifted from my chest like the exhale of a
bench press.

With the pounding of every sprint,
the lingering desire of a woman's affection
was always somewhere visible in the mirage
of the next quarter-mile, always sought after

though never clutched in my bare hands.
I wanted to hold it down against the pillow,
thrust into it with the weight of a blind initiative.

The cardio burned away all my psychic baggage,
and yet the days were followed by months of relentless training
until the blackened cloud of my own ambition
blew itself over the runner's track,
and having collected all the mnemic residue it could bear,
poured itself out over the field and exercise equipment
where I found myself in yet another class of longing.
Every inhale brought with it the desire for the next pump,
and every exhale brought with it an adrenaline-induced
testosterone injection that never found catharsis,
thirsting to be satisfied like a protein deficiency,
until the only presence in the evening weight room
was a featherweight bodybuilder lying under the
pressure of a four hundred fifty pound bench,
and the unshakeable image of an angel
undressing in the outfield, a fly ball
falling from its place upon a cloud
and nesting in the bosom of her naked glove.

JTA City Bus, SS6 to UNF

I.

We bent light across sound waves
rolling down Beach Boulevard,
racing wind twisted vision like Technicolor
as a drunken delinquent and military dog
howled profanity toward domestic authorities.

Sobriety sinks itself into chilled veins, stagnant
under the thin layer of skin upon which
your hairs stand like stones on the now
shivering part of your back and neck-

The sick children coughing at the DMV
now set the tone for your indictment,
the room coloring you chameleon,
a shallow gray settling into the soft
tissue behind your heels and crawling
up the leg, chest and chin until
you are fully engulfed in it;

you are known by your number
and called by anything else. Where
is that bravado that you had only
a few days before?

II.

License revoked, you stand on the corner
of Grove Park and Beach Boulevard
as the wailing screech of the bus's brakes
call your sleeping eyes to attention.

This driver's only known glory is perhaps
his own happiness: a wife, a child,
this job. Perhaps he is a genius
not yet known to the world.

I just want to get to class on time.

I isolate myself in a seat; these walls
can't hold my intruding bitterness.
I broke the law. That truth
begins to settle on my mind as
I watch the city pass by. The city is
a cavern in which the dead revel in
their deadness, a tribute to Hades where
the passive and content are sacrificed for
the benefit of the law, and this road is
a river of souls upon which we ride,
the driver, whose life is unknown to me still,
the great ferryman of the river Styx
to which my lofty and impatient soul waits
to be pushed one way and the other.

Krav Maga

Two months later, they'll make me bow
and beg forgiveness
but my family was the source, cause
and origin behind my intent
to join Krav Maga.

I was heavy with self-defeat,
you could see it in my cheeks-
those fat frowns
my mother loved to squeeze

now burning, disintegrating
by my own efforts. Inner dragons
turned timbers to ashes
in this air conditioned studio-

and who are they
to make me share the room
with pregnant women
and forfeited fathers?

O, and how my mother
claimed her own abuse
when I came home wounded,
as if those scars were her own-

Beat me harder, I wanted to say
to my instructor laughing, I,
smiling through bleeding gums
as blow after blow
rained down over me.

Standing before my mother,
my tongue could no longer explain
the way my heart gained weight
for every pound I lost
as I came home uploading pictures
of my wounds.

That night, those photos spoke
their thousand words
as I tried to convey the way
I loved those blood and bruises.

The Astronomer

Religion was the dusty stoop of a broken down apartment
in New Jersey every Saturday night,
you, seven years old with moonbeam eyes and a yellow nightskirt.

The constellations were your bedtime stories
when your father's sawdust hands
were wrapped around the neck
of a broken bottle,
when your mother was still a labyrinth inside and
came home sweating on November nights.

Your uncle promised you a job at a bar
down in Jacksonville, and
prayer was hoping for food every day,
shelter every night,
and hitchhiking was your pilgrimage.

When you reached Florida it would be
like seeing Mecca
for the first time.

You first saw them when you ran away from home,
clothes stained with mascara and blood.
The sky hung like a black hand over the trees
holding all the stars you had never seen in your life,
modestly reposed over the city and
you said you dreamed of Orion leaning over you,
caressing your naked cheek while you slept
in the dirt outside city limits.

> *You wake up on the outskirts of town*
> *choking as the sand-soaked wind burns you alive,*

27

eyes crusted and caked with sand shells.
Your mother is here.
She is standing by the water
and floating among the seaweed
is a limbless body, yellow and ancient.
She stares as you cling to her shirt with
your head buried in her hips as the police
come to remove the body.
When he approaches your mother he says to
keep quiet
she didn't see anything
you weren't here
and you watch your mother nod her empty head
as the police drive away, consumed by the silence
of the New Jersey streets.

That constellation was there when you woke up
the morning after, around dawn
when the sun held the stars in a baby blue sky and
you looked up to him, waiting for him to stretch
his shining arms down and pull you in.
You watched him fade with the rising sunlight,
pulling you in hot and alive,
swallowing you whole.

To my Brother II

I was tired then,
like a playground grows weary
in winter
and the students romance about recess.

I watched her
in the lunch room,
(a dress,
small sandals)

and approached her
the way a young girl approached you
that morning, dry-eyed
and wanting.

Your lips formed
the familiar "Oh" strung
like a noose
by the letter "N", but
silent-

as if tomorrow
would yield a different answer,
your admirer and I sharing
some new united meaning
together, our footsteps
in unison,

but when we walk back
to our seats,
you'll both be in that
familiar repose

eating on the other side
of the lunch room

never having thirsted
a day in your life,

always more than
a feather's distance
out of reach.

A Girl Named Emily

I.

There's not a rose for you
in this condominium,
just merlot.

We drank it
on the couch, on the bed,
over the kitchen countertop-
we lay flat on our backs
drinking it.

At seventeen years old,
you had something to prove,
the two of us chasing away
our childhoods together,

your girlish charm
blooming, my body
buried like a root
inside you.

It was about virtue
and chastity, the way
we saved ourselves
singing John Legend
in the candlelight,

about fantasy
and voracity,
the way
color comes

with a thousand
different faces

and it was about
your father
by the telephone
waiting for your call,

but it was not
about the two of us,
you and I-
the sheets tossed
and the room turned
on its side, and
the roach smoldering
in its ash tray,
the embers
glowing in your eye,
two bottles of merlot
on the floor drunk
from two separate glasses.

II.

We often spoke of Aristotle,
and the way we wore tragedy
and comedy like masks
around the workplace.

They toasted our better health,
making jokes about our flirtation
as if it were staged. The tragedy

came when you stumbled onto
a scene playing Phaedra,

everyone's faces shifting red
and blue to the song of the sirens
that night, your boyfriend didn't know
what hit him-

Poseidon's creature came in the form
of a five-year conviction. I wonder
when your catharsis came, finally
on the tongues of all your peers?

I heard the story through the grape vine
at the condo, my heart pounding like
a hamaritic wound as I realized
that I was Aphrodite's curse in all of this,

the unspoken stage direction in your guilty
childish step. Lying down on that same couch
again I reflect on the way peripity walks
into life like a messenger pushing a hospital bed
offering up its desperate recount of tragic events,
social order's organs in a disorganized pile,
and the way we try to put those pieces
back together in vain, weeping
over that puzzle's unforgiving chaos.

III.

The girl in the yellow dress
was the way the world knew you,

but I could see a scarlet letter
burning beneath your breast
each time you spoke of home.

You spoke of your father's curfew,
of school books in tiny offices-
because that's where your father taught you-
and you had never known
the world's magnetism, or the way
friendship wraps its arms
around your shoulders and sighs,
the way it never wants to let go.

Later, that same world spat poison
at you from its leafy cheeks;
a world whose poles had reversed
and whose forests had shone
an envious green after having seen
your majestic curves pressed
against its own like two planets colliding.
I'll always remember you as the girl
getting dressed early that Sunday morning,

the sun's fingertips gently stroking your skin
as you told me of all the places you had never been,
delicately clipping your bra-
of all the things that you had never seen,
sliding on your blue jeans-
looking back at me over your shoulder
as if I hadn't noticed,
turning your head so I could never see
your divine, impassionate tears.

Red Room (Photography Development)

The building's tired tonight-
the evening's dimmed its wavering embers
on a plume of purple smoke.

Company's a shimmering frame
on the wall, a thousand years fermented
like a suggestion for the evening,

for every evening when the Polaroid
finds itself burning fuel into a
slow summer heartbeat again.

In the red room, it's always a photo of us
in a foyer under the eye of a ticking clock,
its face reflected in the silver of our wine glasses.

You leaned into me and whispered:
for every vineyard there's a vintage-
as the flavor of the wine slipped

from the brim of your lip and onto mine.

Jack & Coke

The room's a glass

the way
we crack the ice
drinking whiskey

and the lamp's dim,

the way
my single-malt
language
slips its way
down your throat

and burns,

the way
my arm's
wrapped round
you

and your skin's
like amber
sparkling carbon
in that glass,

the way
we mix together
in conversation
on the gentle eve
of our next
round.

Pharaoh's Tomb

This room is a desert in which
the heat brings me to the forefront
of my awareness and is as lonely
as a sea of sand.

I am wandering in this place,
this place in which I do not
want to be, a place in which I
am lost and alone,
feet buried in the dunes.

She's calling my name
from very far away, and yet
she is right here, so very
vivid with immediacy.

I am a pharaoh and this is
the work that I do: embalming myself
here in this bed, with arms crossed
holding my hooks, yet as dead as I am
this moment continues to be alive.

She is a god that I fear, that swallows up
the whole world with her famine. She is
a swarm of locusts consuming the harvest
of my heart, the way she takes without giving,
knowing no master except her own appetite.

When she finishes, there is nothing left of us.
The bathroom is an oasis in which

I stare at my reflection, a mirage
with which I have become unfamiliar.

I know now what it means to be buried:
being a slave that carries stones to the top
of someone else's pyramid, being whipped
by your own desire and then dying
in the scorching sun, your body covered
by the storms of sand, no one having remembered
the location of your home or the value
of your own name.

To my Brother III

Somewhere in the whirlwind
of your bedroom
there's a storm growing
inside you, a starving bitch
named loneliness

and all the television
programs in the world
can't feed it.
I know the feeling-
I spent Saturday mornings with
my head between my knees
listening to the sound of the Nintendo
humming its somber theme
to an empty room
on "pause".

You came forward
holding the chess board,
your tiny features shifting
into a small request,
but I sent you back into
your chambers sulking,
yawning in all my
arrogant boredom.

How I mourned
that decision
one night in
Nashville, writing
heavy-handed
onto a tear-
soaked page,

imagining you
alone with your games,
you, having set your
pawns neatly in a row,
filled with adolescent
readiness, the rooks
protecting you from two sides,
the knights carrying
you on their backs, the bishops
praying for you
every night,
suckling
at the queen's
breast and
idolizing
that king.

I imagine
all the pieces in black
lying on their sides,
longing to put their blades
to the throat of their
absent, degenerate god.

Religion

We lived in a quiet house
at the end of a long rocky road in Nashville,
a tender sanctuary where the sounds of
the dog sleeping in the backyard and
the hiss of a burned-out cigarette
went unheard.

I was three years old swinging on the porch
with my great grandfather, a living ancestor,
bones hardened like gunmetal from the war
and blood flooding with nicotine,

but he was my religion-
a smile and a round belly kept me going
higher on that early morning swing.
I can remember four-line hymns,
a tone-deaf old man and a little boy
that sounded like Johnny and June at
the Grand Ole Opry, the only sound for miles.

Every day had that Sunday-after-church feeling,
like a weathered cardigan and a used tobacco pipe
until the clouds melted away into an afternoon painting,
that wild Tennessee sky splattered with watercolors
overlooking the hills, and then

as the sun slipped into the ground
I grew out of that old swing,
but Papa could still lift the moon into the sky,
dot the yard with a million lightning bugs
and sing those old songs as if
the soul of the south could never die.

Mother

Mother

We were quite a pair, the two of us
walking the mall in matching overalls,
me feeling safe right under your wing,
my buttons reflecting in the light.

So nice in the nest, you believed,
why should your little baby leave?
I wanted to fly, you know, younger
than most, but wherever I went

you followed, and the result was
morning car-rides spent in warfare
over my grades and decisions.
Don't you know, I screamed,
you can't change me?

Don't you know that a man
is like a wind, beautiful in its inability
to be grasped and controlled?
I said I knew myself, you swore by
your wisdom, we just couldn't
see eye to eye.

Years later,
you hated work but said you loved it,
you suffered slings and arrows
but said you didn't, and I watched you
sit on that couch every night
and grade papers, the TV mocking you
with its bad influences, telling you

you're fine when you're not;
how I hated the decisions you made in
all those years teaching. I learned it from you,
you know, this knack for criticism,
so what can you say to me
when I act out in my own mother's
behavior, telling you to escape

all those bad things, telling you
I love you, telling you I know better
than you do?

The Hammock

The neighbors leave their rocking chairs
to peek over the fence,
trying to get a glimpse of us
smelting our bodies into the crisp
autumn air, the energy between us
glowing red above the fallen leaves.

I hear you whisper to me-
What do you think they're saying?
and I let the words
nothing important
linger on my tongue before
I let them free. I press my head
against your belly, letting the ropes
print crossed lines into my cheeks.

I hear you ask me if I meant what I said.
Everyone's voices have disappeared,
the backyard drained of its color,
the sun stretching its arms over
the backyard, waiting for a response.

I smile and press my head
further into the netting.

Sarah's Triptych: *Moon*

He's the river to her quiet evening,
two feet dipped in water,
little waves splashing along the docks
to a boy in a small cap, head turned to the sky
with eyes reflecting in the moon beams.

His boat bumps against the dock
to a beat, all the worn hymns
from his father's memory come back to him
finishing the knot in his nylon rope.
His lantern's lost its oil, the wind blows
as the candle's smoke makes its shapes.

The home's azure tonight, just
at the other end of the yard-
white panes, blackened inside.
Coming from that back door
her feet bend blades between the grass,
padded noises followed by wood in waterlog
as she takes her place beside him singing:

A boy is grown by rivers,
travl'ing day by day,
one day he's sure to become a man-
look at the mile he's made.

"My oil has always belonged to you,"
she says, filling his lantern. Her home's
chimney puffs its choking puff
as she sees him into the boat,
sees off the dock, sees him travel further
down that winding river, and sees him traveling
to the end of that river
and back again.

Sunny Day

Everyone's raving about the weather today
on social media websites and in the news;
my ears ring to the sound
of their chimes.

The coffee pot calls from the other room,
the kitchen foaming with a bubbling
invitation to the day.
I lift my head from the pillow
and gesture to them-
a reassuring wave,

but the gentle pressure
of the sunlight in bed has me
tugging at the sheets
again. Softly reaching
to the night stand, it grabs
a notebook and an ink pen for me
with its tender rays,
and before the coffee loses its kick
in the kitchen, I take a few minutes
resting in the eye of the day
to lie back and write
these lines.

From Yesterday

She was a handful of dandelions
out of reach in the front seat, and her seeds
floated to the back of that old school bus
on wind blowing through cracked windows.
Seat by seat, I jumped leap frog toward her,
a living library, her backpack filled with leather,
those shining spectacled eyes buried in a good book
on the first day of Kindergarten.

Two pink dimples. Electric neck-
her lips were a warm summer on mine,
her hand perched on the nest of my cheek,
my heart's chirping blue jay calming
as she walked toward her mother at the bus stop,
turning over her shoulder as she went.

Some nights, that young memory
finds its way to my doorstep
in ripened age, its hips curved,
breasts full, dressed vintage.

Between us, we split a cigarillo
and a full bottle of wine,
the air filling with tobacco smoke
and conversation, and maybe,
if I catch its eye the right way,
her memory will hear me wondering
if that grown woman
still carries me with her
like one of her favorite books,
or if there is even a seed left
after all the wind between us
floating somewhere
in the garden of her dandelions.

From Venus to the Willow Trees

A woman blushes in a wicker dress
under the willows of a midnight swamp,

but the symphony's for you-
conducted by the crickets, the egrets,
the splashing of shallow waters
at the river's edge. This vibration's

for last night's performance
when you struck a chord for Venus,
a note that cried out over the chorus
and into the audience. At your
standing ovation, you left the stage
for that woman blushing, the two of you
resting in the mud, letting it sink in around you
as the sky's indigo let free all its
soundless visage.

The swamp becomes the orchestra of your own design,
the constellations holding strings at their chins
in ambitious rest, a note for the sleeping pause
in every cloud, Venus wielding
a baton at the lectern of their center
as the two of you lose harmony
under the willow branches in shadow,
washing tides under a fallen star.

House of Cards

With nothing to do,
I paid the fifty cents
to buy the two of us
a deck of cards
one afternoon

in September, a
transition month.
Nothing gained,
nothing forgotten
between August
and October, I
think.

You cut the cards,
careful not to
let the wind blow
any away,
me, firmly
planted in my chair,
your hair whipping
brunette winter

between us as we
took our hands and
I'm cherry red as you
read my poker face
like you always could-

Valentines Day in
our childhood,
sweets on your desk

from anonymous.
You give them back
to me without blinking,
and return
to the academy.

I'm all in
on three of a kind,
the aces smiling
in their neat row.

You call me
for the first time
in weeks on that
river running red
with hearts, and slapping
the table you finally
show me your
naked hand-

a royal flush, the ace
I was missing at the end
of that alphabetic string,
its arms crossed,
barely amused.

Cooking with Wine

The kitchen is a woman's soft skin
upon which the sun has laid its hand. The day
is alive with light, it cascades in abundance
all around this place. It reflects against
the clean furniture; we are at the center of all
this bliss.

Music plays softly around the room and
gives a face to the moment. It is characterized
by a simple piano, a jazzy singer's voice.
The pan has only just begun to sizzle,
and the distinct pop of the wine bottle
defines the room, gives flavor to more

than just the food we're cooking. You wear
your smile the way you wear your dress, it speaks
volumes to the book shelf of your thoughts; behind
your eyes is a thinking mind. I add the wine to the
base, a plume of steam grows from a satisfying splash.

We're cooking up something good here, something
that brings narrative to the literature of life. There's more
to this room than just the Italian ambiance. We're growing
like the garden from which these ingredients were grown.
We're singing like the emotion from which music sings.

This miracle is as simple as breathing, and within it,
we breathe. We finish the meal as the afternoon covers
the room in shade with its softened glow. Cleaning
the kitchen is made better by a handful of kisses. No day
is forgotten when it's lived like this. We take our place

on the couch with drinks. We live the day like we know what the day needs. As the day turns to darkness, we kiss as if to say we know what the night wants and longs for.

Geisha

The room's turned to black.
There's moonlight in the window
of a geisha's sovereign chambers,

and sakura's in all the darkness:
one for every flame
in her candlelit offices.

Her character's coy;
a blade in the thicket
and a shining floral kimono-

the room's color painted
chemical in the afterimage
of her faded swaying mai.

The client's weighted
with sweating palms
wrapped around the nape

of an iron walking stick,
hung by the power in all
his kingdom's jewelry.

But she's writing the poetry
of his imagination,
her eyesight sharpened

by the edge of two coins being
struck together and igniting a spark
that compliments the flavor of rice wine

and illuminates the seduction
dripping from the blood
painted across her softly pursed lips.

Her face is a blade
piercing the snow
shooting from the darkness.

Anime

Give me costume and a colored wig-
there's religion in this convention's hotel,
the way we bend at the knees,
worship cartoon characters that
demonstrate an animated ideal:

the sexual deviant, the vagrant hero-
give them armor and a wooden staff,
an infectious body and an enchanted life-
they're the reflection of our being,
their souls bound inside us, unreleased.

These Japanese archetypes
are all we know, all we have known
since a young age when attention
was taken away from us by our parents
and we relied on five o' clock
television programs after school

to teach us how to fight our own battles
and express our sexuality-
with a sword too big for our sheathes. That's
the only way to describe overcompensation,
the way imagination consumes you
with the illusion of an illustrated life
as if the fantasy were the boy playing Nintendo
alone in his childhood bedroom, and reality
was the graphic novel that he left in there.

It leaves you wondering, who's the player behind the mask?
A stranger whose father never taught him how to fight,
and whose mother never taught them how to dance.

So when you put all of us in a room together,
behold us in the beauty of your eye
and imagine us like this:
a society of unforgiven dreamers
creating a destiny of our very own,
undressing from the persona of a lottery life,
and slipping into an extravagant outfit
we call anime.

Blue Room (Nocturnal Rhapsody)

The sound of the piano creates notes that
linger in the air above us in this place. Look
at the way they play like smoke, the way they
dance like lovers in a ballroom, spinning
and spinning around the air until they're
made dizzy as if drunk. The dancers are

filled with the immediacy of love, and that's
what love is: immediacy. It builds like a symphony
orchestra and then ends suddenly
with the wave of a baton. Who's the conductor
at center stage, the commander
at the symphony of love?

When you move your lips, the sound
is the soft lyrics that compliment this
song and dance; your words are an admission
to several years of passionate effort. How
immediate this moment is, the two of us
bathed in soft blue light. Like everything
else, our conversation builds and
our emotions heighten until the room is filled
with a swarm of angry noise.

I make accusations and you throw something
hard, we make music with the sound of our pain,
then you say it, and it ends without a word.

Open Mic

We know each other in this run-down bar,
everyone silent in their seats. We don't
have to say a word. We hear each other's
emotions. The beer kicks good. The night
lies low. The bar is a blackened mess, but
no one notices.

The reader on stage commands,
and the audience obeys. They bend
to the sound of his poetry. All around
this venue is anonymity. Where's the
poison of occupation's grasp that
owned us only hours ago?

We are occupied by the thoughts of
the reader, and when his thoughts become
language, we drink knowledge. We drink
it hard, harder than any liquor or old
lingering memory. Art absolves us of
our past. A confession on stage is greater
than a confession in church. Our poetry
is a Hallelujah choir. The congregation
throws their head back with pleasure,

and they know what it means to be saved.

School of the Arts

Your hallways were decorated with
amateur paintings, the work of
aspiring students, and
you filled your auditoriums with
music that held a professional sheen;
the average ear couldn't distinguish
a youth performance from
the city orchestra.

You prepared young hearts
for a liberal career, yet there seems to be
a worldly resistance to the pursuit
of what they call "simply entertainment".
To the fathers that reject anything other than
the pursuit of business: can you explain
this world in anything other than tongues?

We have given a name to the nameless,
a word for every subject without identity,
yet young artists are outcast in a world
that glorifies the material, brings the world
to war over a single ugly gemstone; if only
it were painted with graffiti, then we might

come to an understanding. You are a faction
that processes and manufactures,
but our hearts have language to explain
the fluctuation between the pleasure and suffering
that comes naturally with life,

and in doing so we find liberation from the benign.
We want to paint the world in all ranges of color

while it struggles to realize what we have
already attained- so who are the parents that come
from a war-stained background to make commentary
about our school, a place where
the different arts work together in harmony,
a society of its own where its people have
an understanding of themselves and a love
for the work that they produce?

Utopia

Your streets are paved with the scraps
of new works; they flail in the streets
when the wind kicks. Your walls are hidden
behind the graffiti, each brick signed
by an aspiring artist.

The sound of an instrument plays on every
street corner. You've got a day man on the
violin, you've got a night man on the piano.
The city walks among you when the people move.

The homeless are jobless bastards, but they run this
town. They're all geniuses in their field, they take
to the streets and create masterpieces. Don't forget,
the economy's mad. The ballet in the park made
a million flat!

Everyone's paying out of pocket just to feel.
There's nothing like watching the players put on
their faces and take to the stage, give us that fruit
of life that makes us reflect back on ourselves,

that makes us alive. We're just a bunch of junkies
out here getting fixed on our intellectual pleasure.
Say what you will, but the wealthy sit in their offices
surrounded by shapes and numbers. Their colorless world

is defined by the nature behind which greed exists:
an empty heart that turns the world to business in order
to hide its ugly face and create waste, while the impoverished

paint the world beautiful and throw their possessions
in the streets. Here, the worthless are given worth by
the power of their mind, and their ability to share it
with the world by the works that they create. The city

glows when the world ends, having been given another
reason to take to the page and write about the conversion
of pain to pleasure.

What Art Does

White washed walls in a local art museum.
The people walking by are lost in a haze.
Colors vibrant against the absence of color.
Color moving against the absence of motion.

Something soft plays in his headphones, something
good. He stands before the exhibit. The people pass
as he stands alone with the painting. A colorful splashing
of paint that becomes a portrait of a young woman's face.

Art is a living body. The body controls the senses. His
muscles relax while the body takes control. The piece becomes
the sound of a loud nightclub in the early nineties.
Here he is now, ordering a drink at the bar.

The young woman approaches, tells him her name.
"Did you know that art attacks the heart?"
She plays with a blade at the corner of his mouth.
A young man is subject to the power of emotion.

The strokes in the painting are the flashing of lights
on the dancefloor. The shape of her mouth is a furnace
where the flame of her lipstick burns. Art is a love drunk
bitch, and she gets what she wants. Far away,

a boy closes his eyes in a downtown museum. His heart
is a taxi cab making its way down main street, the lights
blurring as they pass by at sixty miles per hour. After
a long night, he finally goes home.

Oedipus

Thebes

Make your commandments to them
in earnest. It's true, they are
cursed before you, the priest himself
coming to you with the name
of Zeus on his tongue,

but let's hear nothing of Creon's prophecy;
what can we make of it? Just a suggestion for
the perpetrator of this heinous deed,

but we have no way of knowing the face and name
of those who strike pain upon this world,
so how do we come to realize justice, or better yet
find recompense for the anxieties that follow us
from an uncertain and unfortunate birth?

So easy when we turn to the mirror
and observe the face of all our misdemeanors-
we inherited this misfortune, yet what
can we make of all that has come before
this climax, each scene's action, the nature

of willful decision in the face of a prophesied fate?
Without an answer, we find ourselves at the end
of our play, having celebrated with hot needles,
not knowing the difference between destiny
and self-empowerment, our children
in our arms, weeping to some divinity
about the relationship between vision
and the ambient light that gives vision sight.

88 Cents

Nausea swims its way to the corners
of your mouth, tugging on the world's
axis and rolling on the tongues
of a drunken traveler.

There's fungus in these familiar passages,
a toe pressing into the worn footsteps of
the last rotation, a chin pressed down
against the chest, eyes of a grandfather clock
swiveling from each side
watching the withered visions of a dime store
squatting on the end of another paycheck,
humming to the sound of coupons
cut from the fabric of your own clothes.

Isles float by to the rhythm of
misfortune's inharmonic tune,
that ambrosial product singing
to your everlasting hunger, harboring
in the shallows of your gullet,
eyeing each individual minute ticking by
like the guttural moans of Tantalus
reverberating from the interim
of poverty's overwhelming stagnation.

Movement
settles into your muscles and
you find yourself rereading the same two lines
from the indictment on your last bank statement:
a decimal followed by two figure eights,
like two black heads twisting their necks
three hundred sixty degrees and breaking;

like two weeping lovers lying
on top of one another in the silence of their
ghostly offices, dwindling in the requiem
of their own voracious infinity.

Sarah's Triptych: *Star*

They're hushed
sprinting in a forest full of trees,
the wind shakes the leaves
like fingertips through a dirty head of hair,
fleeting footsteps like a
rattlesnake bound in metronome.

There's no time in a mountain
like these, formless creatures shaking
their tambourines
to the beat of the naked runners
whipping through bushes,
eyes cut like diamonds
and sharpened sparks glowing
in the afterimage.

Inertia molds them into
a field plateau at the end of a wood,
the sound of her voice saying,
Let's rest in all the absence.
He pulls her into the circle, chest
twisting in a knot as they wrapped
legs like a tangled vine,

one hand bound to the other,
two ropes tied together
in a hunter's snare and
she loses consciousness lying flat,
eyes trapped in the cosmic cartographer
of her waking mind as he tells her,

We're a dream in all the vanishings,
a world in which one star falls
like a teardrop in a river of constellations,
a ripple vibrating like a thunderclap
across the darkening skyline,
blanketing the lost micro fictions
of our forgotten story; a past
that was never heard from,
a future that was never told.

Velvet Lady

Adolescence was the first thing they stole away,
but they fed me a different kind of youth-
something like a living anesthesia
that became the hallways of my new dorm house,
those sweating white walls
locking my eyes to the ceiling on nights
when my own stomach lulled me to sleep,
and the thought of luxury crawled to my bedside
like a child, and showed me the image of a woman:

money in the form of a velvet lady,
moving casually as she goes,
swaying her hips before Dante,
her dark hair sharp in the winter
that she carries along with her,
eyebrows cocked as if to say
I want you to look for me in the garden,

I want you to suck the venom from my veins.
She is here in the room with me
as I write these lines,
stroking the pen as I go, a presence that
fills the quiet space between my roommate and
the dollar dinners resting on the table
by the tail end of her nightgown,
her crimson voice whispering to the page,
seducing the poetry that gives her life.

We Called it our House

It was two brothers balancing chemicals
between one moment's oxygen and
another moment's hydrocarbons-
on four hundred dollars' rent
and all the new clothes we could buy;

it was dripping air conditioning
mixed with the solemn sound of redemption
running through the halls of our apartment building
like a stream waiting for rain

and it was the absence of a woman's whisper
behind the bedroom door each night,
a ghostly lack of noise crawling along the walls
in a haze, resting without a word
in the silence of every room,

but I think we both knew
it was a lapse in consciousness,
two undergraduates looking for love
in a gram and a ten dollar handle,
two skeletons searching for flesh,
and the marrow in their own bones.

Buzzed

Your buzz was somewhere in the mirror
when I found you, wrapped in a cigarillo
and some old hospital bandages
but it was the flavor that kept me there,
toking on your empty physique
in a dimly lit room. We made love to
those songs together,
somewhere between the bed and
the sleeping fireplace-
but when the smoke cleared
the only music left was mine,
alone with a pile of ash
and a dusty reflection hanging from the wall.

Hoodies & Inhalers

I walked in the footprints of yesterday's contempt,
a young boy lost between two rows
of unforgiving eyes that painted the path
to the back of that old school bus.
Maybe it was the black hoodie
that walked with me down that quiet isle
that reminded me of middle school,
or the chunks of fat hanging from my ego
like a damp rag, or the mop of curls
lost somewhere in a nervous hurricane-
no, that was just the ADHD
raining thoughts over the torn leather seats,

but looking out the back window
of that old, beaten school bus
I could see the memories driving themselves,
riding close behind as they spat fumes
and me, barely able to breathe,
clutching to an inhaler like a lifeline,
a wailing ambulance burning red
in the palm of my hand.

de Sade

You ask for this, you want this.
You return to it every day, this abuse
that you willfully receive. Don't you know

that she owns you,
this nine-to-five job that you brag
to your mother about when she calls you?
From a young age you were prepared
for this. Education was your puberty,
and they told you when you finished college
the satisfaction would be a reward
that would climax from anticipation.

It's the waiting that kills you
isn't it? She knows just how
to play with your emotions, the way
you wait on your knees at the end
of every second week,
receive your paycheck like a cigarette burn,
and let your mistress have her way with you
all the days in between.

The things we do for money. It's no twist
of our wrist to wash the dishes, fold clothes,
flip patties during our freshman year of college.
We like the pain. As long as she keeps feeding
our hunger, we'll keep coming back to it day
after day, letting this world keep beating us
to death, sucking dry all the pleasure we can get
out of that fetish for security and stability.

Sculpture

It's just your standard 8"x11"
problem, one error occurring after another
in an open white space
somewhere in the powdered air
of your lamp lit offices. It's an artist
staring at a block of marble literature
without a chisel, but a tight fist wrapped around
the question of
who this child is going to be,
what romantic algorithms she is going
to overcome or, what fathers may
hold her down by her wrists-
his Redeemer a blackened monolith-
singing choir till dawn when
the sharpened horizon severs the sunrise,
taking the cruel morning's
fresh virginity.

Stained coffee cups and dried ink pens:
having surrendered to the rising sun,
the bags under a writer's eyes yawn
their dissatisfied yawn.
Stretching up, lethargy reaches
for each tired lid, clutching skin
at its chest like the comforter
in a four-poster bed.

Dreaming, that child's lifeless body
lies before the Pantheon.
Her arms lie crossed over her breasts,
one leg limply strewn to the side.
Her father paces in the grass. Nearby,

you kneel bent with one elbow
to your knee, index finger
and thumb pinching your chin,
thinking about poetry, still as stone.

Suicide Note

Maybe I'll do some justice to my predecessors.
As a writer, I have inherited an oven, a shotgun,
and a pocket full of rocks. There's more to this
than just the pen and the page:

behind the poetry there's a functioning mind
at work, playing in the dark areas of the human
experience. You think all this comes from
some divinely appointed talent, that I don't

deliberate over minute details daily? I don't
just stop at a failed relationship, I make art
out of it. I don't just walk past the flower
by the lake in the afternoon sun, I take notes

on it until it is sunk into my flesh. Doing this work
takes a toll on the mind, but you'll still go back
to your job at the office and brag about all your hard work
as the barrel of this gun tinkers around my thoughts,

and the details of the world fall short of the value
of the common man. They wish for a single person
to walk among them and take it all in; turn it into
art and display it for all the world to see
at their own expense.

White Room (Frozen Wushu)

We're dancing in this tundra,
going back and forth in our woes;

how hungry a man's desire can be,
wanting both respect and affection,
it can be contradictory at times but still

persevere. You hate my pride yet dream
of better things. Don't you know it was power
that built this house, that fed your yearning hunger?

We both want things.

Our thirsty spirits go on consuming the world, having
never been tamed by temperance. A war
rages on between the lovers of the world,
a choreographed and destined battle that
ends in solace, but even a bloodstained

field's grass will purify itself of contamination,
and in the winter, the snow will cover the grass
in white, and history will forget the warfare that
ever was, as children play unknowing in the slush.

Self Portrait

I take up my brush and I'm careful
to start with the shadowed areas first.
That's where I put all my memories
of being overweight, and when they
called me names. That's where I put
my parents' screams, and my
video games; the things that hang
in the back of my mind.

I color in some of the lighter shades,
where my old friends are. They're
hard to see but still there, close
to the foreground of my face. I draw
the ears, where I heard my teachers'
instructions; I always loved school
so much, and I color in the nose,
the thing that brings out sharp memories
of foods I've eaten, and of nature.

I draw the lips which touched
a dozen others. Those dirty things-
they're hated by so many, but those girls
don't know I meant the words
those lips spoke on summer nights.
When I draw the eyes, I see her face,
and his. We were such a good team,
the three of us. My lover and my
best friend, we colored the world
together.

I look at the final product, and then
I look at the mirror. This face is
almost unrecognizable after everything.
Yet here he is, the finished product of years
of the world's work, painting each day
into my life as if creating the foreground
of a living canvas. You performed your art,
striking into my life an experience
with every stroke, creating a continuous
portrait, the unmistakable image
which I claim as my own
as each day becomes another layer
on the picture of my memory.

Dream Analysis

Interpret this:
I wake up in an auditorium and she is there,
running away. I chase her into a house. The house
is a labyrinth that I have to navigate.
When I find her, she is too beautiful for words.
For years I do her bidding, and when I confess
my love, she is already married. She shows me
her child, of which I am in awe. At the top
of a flight of spiral stairs, I take care of the child
as if it is my own.

Analyze this:
I am walking with my closest friends. We laugh
and play together. It is late at night, and the moon
is high. I look at the moon. No one is paying attention
but me. I watch as it turns red mosaic, breaks to brittle
pieces as it falls out of the sky. My friends go on talking
unaware as the world collapses, continues to fall
all around us but for some reason I feel safe,
and then I wake up.

I always come awake for these dreams that seem
to follow me everywhere in my life, dreams that seem
more real than taking in a breath of cold air. My eyes
grow wide as I stare in the mirror and remember my dreams.
I just want to know what they mean, and I apply
everything I know about analysis to these vagrant images
in my mind, but the dreams are still far away like the past,
and every event, whether dream or reality is open
for interpretation, and remain illusive till the very last
moment. Even so, these memories blossom like a bud
in the heart of my mind, shine like bright gems
that become the wealth of my life experience.

Jung

All's monochromatic
in windy Bollingen these days,
a grassy field, its lonely bush-
from where I'm standing
the leather patient beds
and desk accessories have all
but left our history's offices.

Father of the psychic,
founder of the mind,
when you turned titan
did you forget about Zurich?
I find myself reading
and rereading those same lines-

For who would bear the whips
and scorns of time,
the oppressor's wrong,
the proud man's contumely,
the pangs of disprized love-

and disappear into the swirling
complex of a purple imagination.

A creative illness, they're calling it.

Creativity, to be of the artistic disposition-
so whimsical, the diction-
and illness; of dilapidation, of
decomposition-
what's to be said of euphemism's compound?

How proudly
young philosophy speaks of
knowledge and its permanence.
Only in my old age
do I know the meaning of shadow-

it casts itself from the trembling flame
on the table in my study, bending
at the edge where the floor
meets the wall. Shape-shifter, that
haunted face of the unconscious.
It knows the curve of your cheek,
the make of your signature cigar.

I reflect back on '09, do you
remember the lecture at Clark?
I say again, youth speaks
so absolutely and proudly of
permanence,
like this photo remains
unchanged on my desk,
yet even paper can burn,
and in the same way, you seemed
to spark up like a fire and ignite;
you burned brightly before my
impressionable youth and then
disappeared like a used up star.

You're gone the way Anna's gone,
though she's tucked snug beneath
her headstone,

but maybe your absence is for the better,
because there's a gap between
you and I, the thing we used to have;
but theory is a bastard that everyone
hates to love, and even though it has
left its stain on this unforgiving earth,
there is a place for our names in
the annex of history, and somewhere in
the future textbooks, there our names
will be, two permanent archetypes tied together,
the only thing between us that was ever
definite to be forever connected.

Finding Freud

I used to know you so well, friend,
your old name still imprinted on the pages
of my memory. You've changed since
we last spoke, now taking the appearance
of a bearded man smoking his long cigar
at the other side of the desk before me.

I love when you ask me questions
the way you never used to know how to;
you don't ask me what the others do,
you go beyond just my name and occupation.
You want to know about the past, about my
mother and father, you want to know about
the things which make me myself.

I lie here on this leather couch writing you.
This is the way we are now, you and I,
me communicating my inward impressions,
you staying silent, absorbing and becoming it all.
Poetry's like that, playing the role of the psychologist,
speaking to me, helping me dig deeper into the ditch
that I call my past. You do the job that a mirror does,
making it easier for me to look into one,
allowing me to acknowledge my past with a smile
and carry it in my heart as I move forward.

About the Author

Tyler Norris was born in Nashville, Tennessee and raised in Jacksonville, Florida. He was trained in creative writing at Douglas Anderson, High School of the Arts which afforded him the opportunity to meet a handful of his favorite writers including Billy Collins, Patricia Smith, Naomi Shihab Nye, and more. Tyler graduated with a Bachelor of Arts degree in English at the University of North Florida. Tyler aims to reveal himself through his work and produce conscious poetry that aims to explore himself and the world he lives in.

www.ingramcontent.com/pod-product-compliance
Lightning Source LLC
Chambersburg PA
CBHW071105090426
42737CB00013B/2495